Echoes

Meditations on the Fly

by James M. McCullough

Portions of this book were previously printed in 2003 under the title *Voelker's Pond, A Robert Traver Legacy.*

Cover Photo: Robert Traver's grandson, Adam, casts across Frenchman's Pond (photo courtesy of Tim Schultz)

Copyright 2018 by James M. McCullough

ISBN: 978-1718644274

To John D. Voelker, rest his soul, for his enduring writings and example,
and, to Frenchman's Pond, a personality of its own, for calling us back time and again, may you stay healthy and wild forever...

PREFACE

I'm not sure why — perhaps it's just that I'm aging — but I'm compelled lately to explore the origins of my life-long obsession with fishing, recalling the practices modeled for me by old men who placed fishing above what Robert Traver (John Voelker) considered the material "baubles" in this world. For some men, as with me, the wider world makes no damn sense — it's upside down — where what matters most is valued least, children and the living earth. Had all men thought like fishermen, we would all have devoted ourselves to protecting the habitats of trout, and the cold, clean water

PREFACE

that sustains them, sharing them with the next generation.

    My father introduced me early on to fly fishing and to many devoted fishermen, most of whom lived quietly, and to Traver, an icon among the fish philosophers, one at home and content in the microcosms of a private backwater in Michigan's Upper Peninsula he called "Frenchman's Pond... for that is not its name." Traver and others showed me a set of priorities, appreciation and fascination with the watersheds that raised him, escaping the fame Ernest Hemingway embraced. Hemingway emerged as a fisherman at the same time, also in northern Michigan, but abandoned the small streams of his youth for a wider world — a world that could never satisfy — moving him from continent to continent and ending in self-destruction. I've taken heed, and though I do fish elsewhere from time to time, my heart and soul remain committed to these waters.

    I've included here essays I hope reflect the values of the men who taught me to fish. Also included are the essays from *Voelker's Pond, a Robert Traver*

PREFACE

Legacy, with a few new photos I hope complement the spirit of both Traver and the places he loved.

James McCullough
Petoskey, 2018

TABLE OF CONTENTS

Preface, v

Essays on the Fly:

    Echoes, 3

    The Credentials of a Fish Car, 7

    The Meanie Remains, 17

    Fish Lies, 25

    No, But Really, 27

    Boat House, 29

    Monsters in the Dark, 31

    A Legacy of Setters, 35

    First Big Fish, 43

    Two-Hearted Hemingway, 47

    The Age We Season, 59

The Voelker's Pond Essays
- Introduction, 69
- The Road In, 77
- The Pond, 83
- The Cabin, 89
- Fishing, Wishing, and Watching, 93
- Cocktails and Cribbage with the Men, 101
- His Justice's Flies, 105
- Gizmos in the Pursuit, 109
- Equipment, 115
- A Witness to the Dancing Fly, 123
- Native Trout and Television, 127
- Changes and Permanence, 133
- A View Into the Upper Ponds, 139
- A Season's Sendoff, 147

Acknowledgments, 155

MEDITATIONS ON THE FLY

MEDITATIONS ON THE FLY

ECHOES

The men who taught me to fish when I was a boy rarely spoke, but when they did, their language leaned poetic, their tones conveyed sensitivities I think, as I push sixty, I finally understand. They were a gangly lot, retired teachers, unassuming attorneys, doctors and laborers whose fathers passed to them the then seldom understood art of casting flies to trout. Some used the same old cane rods we now cherish and fear will break. They grew up in Northern Michigan in Hemingway's day, or if they moved in from somewhere else, they did so knowing their wives would have to adapt to their lifestyles, and that their lives would never be as profitable as in the city. They knew a good deal when they saw it.

ECHOES

In the evenings, they would let me struggle with oversized rubber waders, never laughing or smiling at my fumbling, then saunter me through the dark woods to the bank where they would take turns tying on my tippet and fly. On the river, they might ensure my footing was sound at first, offer a few instructions, hand gestures, perhaps, but mostly they left me alone to find my way through, to fail on my own in the murmuring swirls of current. From their example, I still mostly saunter, drive an old stick-shift Jimmy, wear mostly muted green, aging boots and believe there will be another and another opportunity so long as my luck and legs hold out. One by one, they have passed, some decades ago, even my father, many winters past.

They're echoes now.

Many times at night, I go to the river for voices that can't be heard. They are preceded by sunset, the far off whistle of whippoorwills, the crackling of nighthawks so high above as to be invisible, and the lovely processional of mayflies. When hours afterward, a blanket of spent flies speckle the water

MEDITATIONS ON THE FLY

in the moonlight, in the deepening silence, I seek out liquid ringlets in reflections that reveal the sipping of secretive trout. I'm mostly alone, but last summer on the Au Sable, when I was not, I heard men sludge home in the dark, smelled their cigars wafting downstream to me while the largest fish sipped silently, only their concentric wakes revealing them.

I wish less and less to speak to others about rivers and trout because it engages us in language that falls inevitably into the jargon men use to include themselves in the fraternity of fishermen. I leave conversations guilty of abasement. So, instead, I prefer my time in the muted presence of one other at a time who shares my sentiment, a long time friend with whom smiles and nods convey the conversation.

I once read the poetry of Native American writer N. Scott Momaday, whose phrase "the wake of nothing audible" has never left me. I think we understand each other.

ECHOES

As I stare upward at a lone mayfly ascending, I realize, somewhere in the past, someone loved its ancestors enough to capture and study them, name them in Latin, the family, genus and species. Their words remind me of the Catholic mass of my youth, when in the hard pews, below the gory Stations of the Cross, I escaped into daydream as the inscrutable ancient language assuaged me with its rhythms. When spoken slowly, sincerely, the words for mayflies become a liturgy: *baetis, hiemalis; ephemeridae, hexagenia, limbata; ephemeridae, ephemera, guttulata.*

And my favorite, both for its sound and the memories it evokes of the emerging warmth of summer, the Latin name for the sulphur dun, a tiny, delicate yellow creature that emerges in late May on Michigan streams: *ephemerellidae, ephemerella dorthea.*

It is deep winter now. Summer is in my dreams. I listen for the language of the river, and all the creatures in it. Their words whisper: *ephemerella, ephemerella, ephemerella, dorthea.*

THE CREDENTIALS OF A FISH CAR

Fly Fisherman Magazine sponsors an annual Robert Traver (John Voelker) Writing Contest that I'm not interested in — because I decided, what do they know — yet as an extension of the contest one year they wanted to select a photo of the ideal "Fish Car," the title Voelker gave his equipment-laden Jeep.

So, after crashing overgrown brush, slamming on a rock so hard my hand hurt on the stick shift, and fording a beaver pond in the spring of that year, I shot an image of my bruised up and decidedly unsexy Subaru Legacy, canoe on top, at Frenchman's Pond, Voelker's secret brook trout

THE CREDENTIALS OF A FISH CAR

Shangri-La. How much more fish car could you want? Then they announced the winning image: some Gucci-ish, shiny Land Rover or such, gilded with rod racks and other state of the art who-ha, a suburban notion of what fishermen should drive to the river.

Sorry guys, that's not a fish car.

A fish car earns credentials, including a history of fearless attempts to reach barely accessible waters, dings from such attempts, a standard shift, and the love and gratitude of the owner — not for its value or appearance, but for its faithful companionship, longevity, and partnership in the pursuit of backwoods access. Fish cars have stories. The Subaru at the pond earned its place in the lineage by taking me on countless occasions through brush and muck, and never getting stuck. It took me at least half a dozen times to Frenchman's back when there was no guarantee we could make it through the rock and beaver dam fortified two track (before a neighbor "improved" the road with a bulldozer). It took me faithfully on thousands of miles of two track over the course of ten years, and in the end, the motor still ran well, but it drove funny so couldn't be sold for use. I called a scrap metal guy to take it away. He said he'd give me a few hundred for it, so I agreed, but when he put the lift under the car to tow it away, rather than lifting it, the rusted frame crushed under its own weight. I'd been driving an accordion, and almost had to pay him to take it.

That was a fish car.

In my family, the tradition began when my father bought a forest green International Harvester Scout II, the original version, before they made them with cheaper steel that rusted quickly. It didn't take long for the Scout to earn its credentials. In the fall, he'd load it with dogs and shotguns, and in the summers, my father loaded it with chains and straps, baskets, axes, hatchets, a machete, camping equipment, the standard waders, rods, stacks of flies and a two-day supply of dry food and drinks, just in case. Then we would take off.

THE CREDENTIALS OF A FISH CAR

The author and the Scout

It was the Scout that took us to Frenchman's when Voelker was still alive, and in it we ambled all over the north, fishing and grouse hunting, exploring up steep embankments and down puddle-rich two-tracks in the days when we could saunter around in the Pigeon River Forest or the Upper Peninsula all day without seeing a soul.

One spring, dad and I tried to find new access to an unfamiliar trout stream, hammering down a wet, vegetation-clogged two-track until we came to a puddle about thirty feet across. We stopped, his discretion being the better part of valor, until I convinced him to take a serious run at it. In those days to get a fish car into four wheel drive you had to get out and lock the hubs, like some crude earthbound preparation like going to light speed. "Lock the Hubs, we're going through," we'd say.

So, I hopped out, twisted the locking mechanisms on each front tire, and jumped in smiling, proud of my father's daring, and braced for what was to come. He backed up a ways to get momentum, popped the clutch and we raced forward splashing and surging about half way, then sank, spinning, soaked to the floorboards. The enormous puddle was not a puddle at all, but a swollen, sandy-bottomed stream affording zero traction. We had to hike a half mile back to the gravel road, then north for several miles before seeing another car that took us up the road to Afton — a town composed of a bar, an old gas station and the gas station owner's house. Dad convinced the reluctant owner to tow us out with his Scout.

The adventures continued like this, until I was twenty, and loaned dad's Scout to use for a year,

THE CREDENTIALS OF A FISH CAR

so I could head back and forth to college in Ann Arbor, and so I could spend my autumn weekends grouse hunting and summers fishing. But I was not a motor-head. In fact, I was an idiot who did not remember he had to change the oil at least once in a while.

When I killed his fish car, it was only twelve years old with a promising future. I was returning in the twilight from hunting north of Harbor Springs with Fat Flora, our English setter, when it threw a rod like a missile into the block, and I ended up gut-sick on the side of Pleasant View road, fretting over how to explain, until a state trooper came by, admired Flora and my three grouse, then drove me home. When I told my father what had happened he looked wounded. I still feel guilty and ashamed, imagining that with proper care the old Scout could still be alive today.

I now own his third fish car, anointed by my father in his final years, and entrusted to me before his passing from pancreatic cancer. It is a forest-green stick-shift Jimmy, as close in kind to the old Scout as he could find. He would have, but couldn't buy a Scout. The International Harvester truck division went belly up years before. They made their vehicles too well.

Like the old Scout, dad's Jimmy has only two doors, a tape player, AM/FM radio I never turn on, and crank windows. It's currently thirteen years old. In that time, he drove it only 13,000 miles, having weakened beyond the ability to farm, fish or hunt, and thus having nowhere to go.

Now that it's been mine for several years, it smells like a blend of wet waders; wet dog; deer, duck and grouse carcasses; ice fishing minnows and mildew, with just a hint of my father's old smoking habit. The interior roof is adorned with one hundred flies of all shapes and sizes, a result of boredom one afternoon. The lever to set back the driver's seat is missing; the right front fender is held together with zip-ties, and the back, top brake light has been knocked off from me hauling up Dad's old Sawyer canoe by myself too many times. The canoe is also forest green, flat bottomed, forty five

THE CREDENTIALS OF A FISH CAR

years old and heavy as a blacksmith's anvil. We call it "The Meanie" for its weight, and it remains a fixture on the fish car most of the summer and fall.

I dread the day I have to lay the Jimmy to rest, but rust is having its way. It's earned its soul, and remains one of only a few possessions I treasure from my father. It's not a car, it's a fish car, a character in my life, a conduit to the old glowing stories of father and son together, carrying all they needed with them on the way to new waters.

Postscript:

This fish car died in the winter of 2016, hit from behind at 60 mph, rolled and totaled — so its final act was to save my life. I walked away through the shattered windshield.

MEDITATIONS ON THE FLY

Death of a fish car

THE MEANIE REMAINS

MEDITATIONS ON THE FLY

THE MEANIE REMAINS

A mix of twenty-somethings, some married, most not, relax on the deck of the log cabin we'd rented in Vermont during my Masters' program at Middlebury College, sauntering from *Hamlet* and *100 Years of Solitude* into a discussion of the nature of love. The mood was light as the sun set, chicken on the barbeque, when we landed on the question: Can you truly love a thing.

Yes, I contended. You can. I love my canoe.

You love a canoe.

Yes, I do, in fact, I said, because it was true then, and even more so today, over thirty years later.

THE MEANIE REMAINS

It's hard to believe I was talking about *The Green Meanie*, an 18½ foot, flat-bottomed river canoe, a wide-beamed fiberglass vessel, punishingly heavy, but stable enough to stand in, highly maneuverable despite its length, and steady as an old friend.

I was seven, when my father made the trek from Petoskey to the Sawyer Canoe Company in Oscoda, where he purchased four laminated beavertail paddles, now worn at the handles and chipped at the paddles, and two canoes: the lovely, cane-seated, cedar-ribbed *Pipsissiwa*, and the then unnamed, sturdy and more utilitarian *Meanie*.

My first memorable voyage in the latter, when I was ten, took my father and me along the forty-mile inland waterway. We launched from Conway, paddling across Crooked Lake through the locks, down the Crooked River to Burt Lake, where we beached on property that by now no doubt is developed. I recall the evil hisses of an aggressive swan whose territory we had invaded, and how that evening an enormous snapping turtle dug a hole to lay dozens of eggs, covering them up with sand. We heard raccoons that night, and woke to see they'd dug up and devoured every egg.

That day we crossed to Burt Lake State Park where we set camp, exhausted, especially my dad who'd done most of the paddling. Afterward, the waterway would take us up the Indian River to Mullet Lake State Park where I saw the longest, fattest and fastest green snake ever, and when I grabbed at it, it snapped back, leaving a half moon of tiny punctures in the crook of my thumb and forefinger. From Mullet Lake we made the Black River and the locks in Cheboygan where mom picked us up.

Throughout grade school, every year on my birthday in May, my parents would pull me out of school, and we'd float the Bear River; we would float the Au Sable too, each summer when we rented the river cabin at Whippoorwill on the Holy Water. I recall an overnight family trip with relatives and friends floating down a stretch of the mainstream, how it rained, the coons broke into our food, and how the son of a family friend was dubbed "Moose Nose" for his constant, reverberant nose-blowing, echoing in the perfect silence of the cedar swamps.

Every summer we'd rent the big white house at Nickie's Silver Birch, a collection of cottages in Walloon Village, and our cousins would come from Illinois, Texas and as far as Washington State. We'd take the Meanie out on the lake, fishing or gunnel jumping, which is akin to log rolling, where my brother and I would balance with one foot on each gunnel, and try to rock the other into losing his balance, splashing into the lake. It's one of those idiocies that later in life make you wonder how you did not split your head open and drown. Then, we'd flip her upside down and sing in the echoing air pocket underneath.

I'm flooded with memories: the time my friend Fred Brill and I thought we could float the west branch of the Maple, but found beaver dams every hundred yards, having to carry the canoe over one after another, until all I could say was, "Damn."

MEDITATIONS ON THE FLY

And floating the Bear too early in the spring, running into ice-jambs, and scooting on top with our legs out of the canoe, but our butts in. And duck hunting every fall at dawn; fishing for bluegill every spring, and floating the North Branch of the Au Sable where we rent a hundred-year-old cabin most summers. Hauling her through the woods with my daughter Madison when she was six trailing behind, hoping to catch brook trout upstream of a hidden beaver dam. I can see her little body, torquing on the paddle to spin us around. And my older daughter Meghan, taking photos with Ripley the English Setter lying between us in the bottom of the boat.

My friend Tim Tebeau christened her The Green Meanie after we hauled, pulled and pushed her though woods, up rooted paths and over vertical hills in Ontario's Lake Superior Provincial Park in search of mythically large brook trout. It took all day just to portage half a mile to the first lake. I have pictures of us completely wheezed out, red-faced and sweat-drenched.

THE MEANIE REMAINS

The author, with Ripley, in the Meanie

The next year, I discovered "McCullough Lake" on a map of northern Ontario and talked my friend David Payne into a quest for that wild destination, which we found required lugging the Meanie uphill through the woods for half a mile, to our complete exhaustion, only to find a house and dock across the lake.

The Meanie. I can see her out the window, even as I type this, in the backyard, upside down, the scarred and patched underbelly with its dripped epoxy from my failed attempt to fiberglass the stern that had worn thin from beaching it a thousand times. She's all scarred and ugly, with a duct-taped bow because I'd dropped her after rotator cuff surgery, thinking I could lift her onto the truck.

I kind of like the look now. The stern is held together with a tacked on bicycle seat, and the seats are cracked underneath. She's where I am now — the handsome days far behind me, but still afloat; I look in the mirror and say screw it; those who love me, those who I love, they transcend all this. It's all deeper than this.

So, can we truly love a thing? I still say yes, if we find where the love is. It's in the intertwined narratives of our lives. From them we discover the things from which we cannot part, the wedding rings, the grandmother's shawls, the photos. We try to pass them down the generations as evidence we were here, that we lived, we adventured, loved, suffered and prevailed. When we hold them in our hands, we feel our lives. That's how it is with the

THE MEANIE REMAINS

Meanie when I'm gliding over the surface of placid waters, past sunset, the gentle grip of my paddle, a touchstone to indelible moments of my life.

FISH LIES

I'm maybe seven, fishing on a dock on Walloon for small rock bass with a long pole, dropping worms into crevices between the boulders when an enormous, bearded man pulls up in a powerboat and ties off, hops out with the largest bass I'd ever seen. He hands it to me and says, "Go tell your parents you caught this." So, I do, and to their disbelief. Thus, I joined early into the fold of fish-liars, a weakness I have long since abandoned. I know why men do it, and among them, over the years, I have met those who all their lives will need a warning affixed to their caps:

$$Truth= -10''/fish/tale.$$

NO, BUT REALLY

NO, BUT REALLY

The family was invited to the north branch of the AuSable to fish on opening day with some friends of my parents who owned a log cabin build in 1904, with screened in bedrooms with beds suspended on chains, where my own family visits most years, even now. You can hear the river below as the bed slowly lulls you to sleep in the cool breeze. But not that opening weekend.

It snowed.

No one except I wanted to fish. With no hatch and a cold wind, I walked upstream and fished back down to the cabin with a muddler minnow, a streamer fly with a cut deer-hair head, gold band on the hook and brown feathers that made it look like a sculpin minnow. I caught nothing until, just

NO, BUT REALLY

about ready to give up, I swam the fly along a log, letting it swing away at the end when a lovely eight-inch brook trout struck.

Everyone asked if I'd caught a fish, but no one believed me when I said I did.

MEDITATIONS ON THE FLY

BOAT HOUSE

Most Augusts, my parents rented the river cabin at a place named for the evening call of the nocturnal bird, "Whippoorwill." The river cabin was more contemporary, but on the bluff above the river, an historic turn of the twentieth-century log lodge (our Trout Unlimited group would gather there every year), stood aside a kitchen and dining cabin, but another smaller, private cabin was owned by Theodore "Rip" Van Winkle, who I loved, and who understood me immediately. He instructed me with the fly rod, and later wrote to me beautifully in the inscription on a copy of "The Old AuSable," a gift for my wedding day. The local chapter of Trout Unlimited was co-named after him when he passed away.

BOAT HOUSE

This is where I first learned to fly fish, in the trout-rich "holy" waters of the AuSable river, as they are known, a stretch of river where no trout can be killed, and only fly fishing is allowed.

At Whippoorwill, past the old log lodge, down the stone stairs, past a trout pond and the sloping grass lawn, an old boathouse sagged on cedar posts, just upstream from the river cabin. The old men spoke to me of a mythically large "boathouse fish" that lived there — a lunker trout no one had ever caught, and at night as I lay in bed, a leviathan's shadow moved in my imagination.

MONSTERS IN THE DARK

"Watch for the muck monster," my father said as he disappeared into the night, heading upstream, leaving me on the bank above a deep river bend. I'm maybe eleven, could barely make out a trace of the river's reflection, and I had no sense of distance across the opaque bend in the moonless, overcast, night-fall.

I shuffled my feet down to the bank, first ankle deep, touching my toe in front of me with each inch, to check depth, and waited alone as my father had told me, for the hex hatch to emerge, the giant Michigan mayfly.

It was my first time night-fishing, and I could not see a thing. The current made no sound, slow and flat. I scooched a bit deeper until the surface reached my anxious knees, and my ankles tucked into muck.

I stopped. Certainly, the water would be over my head somewhere out there, the muck bottom slipping suddenly into the depths. I imagined water filling my rubber waders, floating me away.

A half-hour of solitude passed in the boredom tinged with dark imaginings when a burst of water shocked me to my groin: a giant trout chasing an emerging fly above the surface. I'd never seen such a monster. Then, a minute later, another rip of the surface, violent and frightening, and others, upstream and across from me, beyond my longest cast. I would have to move closer, deeper, and cast blindly upstream and across; the fish were even farther out.

But the bottom drops off out there.

Four or five times I tried to raise my courage, slid one foot, then the other, closer to the drop off, the large, gaping mouths and teeth, concluding, finally, I could drown; I would not be able to cast far enough; my fly would drag and not float

MEDITATIONS ON THE FLY

naturally, and if I could cast far enough, I'd snag on the other side, or hook my head, and every excuse except the full admission that at the bottom of it all, I was terrified to catch one.

A LEGACY OF SETTERS

MEDITATIONS ON THE FLY

A LEGACY OF SETTERS

I am more than fortunate that many of my passions are deeply connected to the northern habitats of my childhood, and their wild, living things. Then there are also English setters, whose powerful hunting instincts are genetic conduits for those natural, primitive impulses I share with them, and that have directed me always toward solitude, water and woods.

My grandfather owned setters, and must have felt the pull, though he was a bit more of a dandy than an outdoorsman. But not so my father who left Northwestern after med school to follow Hemingway's path from Oak Park, where my mother grew up, to the then remote Petoskey, Michigan. Something like instinct compelled these families from that place, northward, eventually bringing them together. Hemingway's younger sister, Sunny, befriended my mother, and her son became my father's constant friend and hunting partner, sharing his cabin, "bird camp," with us from the time I was twelve. In photos as in my memories from those years, the dogs are as often the focus as the men.

My father introduced me early on to setters, and welcomed me to the world of shotguns and autumn woods once I was old enough to follow him through swamp edges and aspen swales of Emmet and its surrounding counties. At thirteen I owned my first 20 gauge and the right to walk with the men every September and October. The sharp aroma of browning bracken fern will forever evoke a lifetime of autumnal memories.

He owned six setters in his days from his childhood, four in my lifetime, the favorite of which, Flora (Lily of the West), lived sixteen years, most of them with me as her primary companion. I was five when we brought her into the family and a junior at University of Michigan when she passed.

MEDITATIONS ON THE FLY

She had been my one constant friend through the turmoil of my youth and long adolescence.

I grew up in the 1960's and 70's on the edge of town next to a bird sanctuary that led to the steep ridges of the Winter Sports Park, then the Bay View woods where Flora and I would search in the evenings for grouse and woodcock. I believe no relations with dogs run deeper than partnership in a single cause, and no cause runs deeper than such instinctual pursuits.

The author as a boy, with Flora

A LEGACY OF SETTERS

I spent most weekends and evenings after school in the river basins, thorn-apple thickets and the edges of fields where grouse came to feed. Fat Flora, we called her, would waddle, wasting little time from pointing one bird to the next. She was known, though, for hunting on her own, often on the wrong side of the river. We loved her for her imperfections.

Once in college, every autumn weekend I would drive home from Ann Arbor, pick up a gallon of apple cider, sandwiches and plat maps, let Flora in the Scout II, and choose a direction. Between hunting stints we'd amble the two tracks, listening to the Michigan game on AM radio, her head on my shoulder.

When I came into my own family and the children began growing up, Lisa, my wife, suggested it was time for a dog. We drove to Essex, between Charlevoix and Traverse City (less a town, more a dirt crossroad), where we met Jim Ruster whose breeding of setters was spot on — a gorgeous male named Scotch — orange and white, and Star, a tricolor, deeply ticked with black and orange. When we first saw the litter, Ripley wobbled away from the others to us and we knew. We were fifth in line, though. Jim did us the kindness of convincing the woman ahead of us — who would never hunt and wanted only a pet — to take another puppy so we could bond with Rip.

She became my hunting and fishing companion and a great canoe partner. Every summer, as I paddled or cast upstream on local trout waters, she would lie quietly or swim beside or behind me. Though from time to time I would catch her foot with the fly line, we had a system and an understanding. We communicated easily and often. Though many of my former stomping grounds are gone to development or no trespassing signs, every fall we'd escape as much as we could to what remains. We had some magic days, such as sunny September afternoons catching brook trout on the fly, then evenings hunting the river valleys.

We have had thirteen seasons together now. With deep gratitude and sorrow, I am seeing her passing into her final stage of life. She has developed hip dysplasia and needs help lifting up her back end. I am torn up, but coming to terms. Dog lovers, like all pet owners, know when we first bring them into our lives, we also bring inevitable heartbreak; yet, we do it anyway.

Postscript:

Ripley passed away quietly in my lap; two years later, the lovely miss Layla has come into our lives.

MEDITATIONS ON THE FLY

Miss Layla, in the Meanie

FIRST BIG FISH

FIRST BIG FISH

When I was thirteen my father bought me a new fiberglass rod to replace the whippy Phillips I began with. By then I'd learned to fish upstream with dry flies, but had not yet hooked one of the big nocturnal brown trout the adults told stories about. I would try when Dad took me to a second camp at Ranch Rudolf on the Boardman River during the brown drake hatch.

I don't remember who instructed, but remember clearly the last night, when the conditions were muggy and still, an older man dropped me alone at sunset on my own stretch of deepening water. I sat on a log, breathing in the cedar-scented air, watching waxwings feeding above the river until the sunlight receded to the west and Brown Drake

FIRST BIG FISH

mayflies appeared, smaller trout rising to them first. As the sun vanished over the horizon, a healthy rise popped by a log in front of me. I cast and caught a fine, foot-long brown trout, so I knew I had a good fly pattern.

No moon rose. As stars appeared, I waded in darkness, upstream, until a tremendous gulp resounded in the tight cedars. I followed the sound blindly until the current ran up to my chest at the back of a deep pool.

I heard the gulp again, about twenty feet upstream, and half afraid I'd catch it, cast directly up the center of the run. I heard him rise, triggering me to set the hook and feel the line-halting heft of the fish that turned and ran directly at me. I stripped in slack line until I caught up with him as he shot back and forth violently at my feet, waving my heavily bent rod. In a panic, I reached out, grabbed the line, and it snapped.

They spent so much time teaching how to hook a big fish, no one told me what to do if I did hook

MEDITATIONS ON THE FLY

one. I'm still surprised no one came running, the way I had let out a groan.

TWO-HEARTED HEMINGWAY

MEDITATIONS ON THE FLY

TWO-HEARTED HEMINGWAY

Having regained a hazy consciousness I first noticed the poster on the wall at Munson Hospital's outpatient program for psychiatric illness; on it were the faces and names of twenty or so historical figures who suffered mental disorders yet made significant contributions to society. A number of them were writers: Hermann Hess, Joseph Conrad, Charles Dickens, Ralph Waldo Emerson, Virginia Woolf, Sylvia Plath, Ernest Hemingway. Then it occurred to me how many had succeeded in committing suicide, most notably to me, Hemingway, and I recalled how his father, Dr. Hemingway, his sister Ursula, his brother Leicester, and granddaughter Mariel all were lost by their own hands.

Though we cannot say for certain, Hemingway's increasingly labile behavior, particularly in the final years of his life, is widely considered evidence of accelerating bipolar disorder compounded by alcoholism, and, I would add, the crude medical care that was the standard of psychiatric practice in the late 50's. In his condition, at that time, he was bound for self-destruction that today is preventable. But if he were properly treated, would he have been the Hemingway who avoided death in Italy, survived two plane crashes in Africa, was drawn to wars and the danger of enraged bulls in Spain, angled for monster billfish in Cuba and transformed the literary world with his Pulitzer and Nobel Prize-winning writing? And would it matter?

What a life; what accomplishments we say. But now, despite his global, iconic image and lasting adorations, I can no longer admire so much as empathize. All I can see any more are the consequences of a frenetic life, the wake of destruction, and an inevitable, downward spiral to the morning he ended it with a shotgun on his forehead in the lobby of his home in Idaho, July, 1961, two months after I was born. He was 61. Our lives overlapped, but briefly, and now, as I approach my 60's, I must say he haunts me.

Where I live, Petoskey Michigan, Hemingway's life is celebrated — at Hemingway Society conventions, in pictures on restaurant walls, on historical markers in Horton Bay and in the local knowledge that Hemingway drank, boarded, married, fished and emerged as a writer here and there. At Windemere, his family cottage on Walloon Lake, hangs a sign on the old outhouse that jokes, "Hemingway Sat Here."

Perhaps because they were both from Oak Park, Illinois, my mother befriended Ernest's youngest and evidently closest sister, Sunny Miller Hemingway, after my family moved to Petoskey in 1962. She was a figure in my upbringing, though in truth, she scared me when I was young with her powerful presence, strong delivery of opinions, and untamed white hair. But after reading the short story, "Last Good Country," I couldn't help but imagine her as a child with her older brother, running away in the woods, perhaps behind the farm near Walloon where my father kept his garden.

Like Ernest, she was a character, though of lesser fame. I remember being alone one night at home, perhaps I was ten, when I answered the phone to Sunny's voice. She had called to invite us out to the cottage for a swim in the dark, with the loose cocktail speech with which I was familiar. As nervous children do sometimes, I tried to weasel out of the invitation with a ridiculous fib. "I don't have a bathing suit," I told her.

"You don't need a bathing suit!" she shrilled, and the image of myself standing naked on the beach with her shuddered me to the toes. I was able to escape with the simple truth that my parents were out, and I was far too young to drive.

I also recall, when I was in middle school and a bus boy at the Chimney Corners, Sunny came in and called me over. "Jimmy, go get me a drink."

MEDITATIONS ON THE FLY

"I can't," I told her, "I'm not old enough."

"Oh, forget it," and she tossed the water from her glass on the floor and pulled an airplane bottle of liquor from her purse.

After Sunny passed away and her son, Ernest Hemingway Mainland inherited Windermere, he told me she had kept it "like a shrine" to her older brother. And that was how he was treated in my own household, particularly by my literary mother who would quip, "There is your Hemingway for today!" whenever — and it was frequently — his name was referenced on television, in the paper or in magazines.

I was expected to read the *Nick Adams Stories* as a boy, and was captivated by the descriptions of the rivers, lakes and landscape I knew, and I imagined myself as the young Hemingway crossing Walloon Lake and walking up Sumner Road with a fly rod to fish at Horton Creek. I imagined myself as Nick, hiding from the law in a hidden patch of first growth trees that felt like a church to him, and from him I learned to yearn backward for a northern Michigan wilderness that had been slipping away even in his day and has been overrun in mine.

Like his father, Dr. Hemingway, my father, also a doctor, battled depression, yet took time to introduce me to the rivers and streams Ernest fished and referenced in his stories. Dad became best friends with Sunny's only son, Ernie Mainland, who remains a kind presence in my life. From the time I could hold a shotgun, dad and Ernie took me grouse hunting in autumn, sometimes spending nights in Ernie's cabin we called "bird camp," deep in the Pigeon River Forest. Every October from my early teens until my late twenties, the men would escape there for a week. Stafford Smith, a local restauranteur, would drive his catering truck down the two-tracks to the cabin, and the families would come out for feasting and hunting the last day of camp. I remember how when he was unshaven, Ernie looked hauntingly like his uncle. Time passed, the cabin was sold, but their friendship endured, and years later Ernie visited every morning as my father declined from pancreatic cancer. He was the first person I called outside the family, when Dad passed away.

But of all the coincidences, the most significant to me is that I live with bipolar disorder, having endured intensifying patterns of illness escalating from adolescence into my forties when I was at first diagnosed inaccurately and prescribed a chain of improper psychopharmacological prescriptions — 26 separate meds in all — including in the end a nightly depressant Ativan, which was not recommended for those with alcoholic histories like mine, and daily maximum doses of Aderall, an amphetamine. Within months, I shot into a full blown manic episode, an overdose, and a long walk in the winter I only partly recall. Luckily, my wife tracked me down with the police and EMT's. Twenty more minutes, according to a neurologist, and I would have joined Hemingway in his manner of death.

In this way, I understand early self-medication with alcohol and the cycles of intense productivity and deep depression Hemingway endured

— sometimes driven and clear on the brink of mania, other times spiraling into darkness. Doctors could not save him with their crude measures and he died violently; I am now under the care of a competent doctor, stable and productive, thanks to the miracle of proper pharmacology, supportive family and the solace of a life outdoors.

In his most anthologized Nick Adams story, "Big Two-Hearted River," we find tenderness for a deeply, psychologically wounded Nick who seeks peace through the healing act of fishing alone in a romanticized Upper Peninsula stream. But in that story, Nick never addresses his demons, and leaves them in the symbolic swamp for another day, one neither Nick nor Hemingway himself ever saw. Ernest had already left northern Michigan, writing from memory in Paris, only returning once, briefly, we think, then never again. Many believe he wanted to hold still the idyllic images of youth. I believe it would be too painful to see the wildness of his boyhood world gentrified. Yet, ironically, he was a summer person. Locals have called him a tourist, a "fudgie" (tourists buy fudge here) who only endured one winter up north.

Perhaps it is pointless to consider what might have been, but I can't help it, wondering, if Hemingway could have quit drinking, if he sought rejuvenation in the rivers of his youth so he might recapture and heal that young man, Nick, could he have survived the swamp? Could he have learned to age gracefully, accept his naturally waning powers, his diminishing physical and sexual prowess, and creative energies? I heal him in my imagination, so he could have written reflectively, remained married and been a constant presence for the children he brought into this world, especially his son who died of alcohol poisoning dressed as a woman in a Florida jail.

But with his chemistry, he had to run.

I see him running from the pain of the inevitable deterioration of a wild Michigan landscape he had loved, running to preserve his idyllic childhood in memory. I see him running because, in the end, like so many who know the intoxication of manic energy, he was born for destruction, always leaving, from continent to continent, drawn by the intensity of adventure. I can speak of mania: it's the running itself, the wild hunt, the more and the more of it. To run, he traded the fly rod of his youth in Nick's quiet streams for safari in Africa where he communicated with the natural world with a high caliber rifle, and in Cuba with large-arbor spin rods pursuing bigger and bigger marlin.

To me, this choice is metaphor for a division in our two-hearted selves, one of which can never be satisfied, and which, without the other, issues in the beginning of the end. He would run for the rest of his life on a razor's edge from which he could not step down.

If he remained in northern Michigan, as a dry fly fisherman, might he have found peace? And if he had, would he have been the icon, Hemingway, the man so many admire without imagining the horror

MEDITATIONS ON THE FLY

his fourth wife found in the foyer of their home that morning in July.

    Still, I pretend, if I can heal, so might he.

THE AGE WE SEASON

MEDITATIONS ON THE FLY

THE AGE WE SEASON

I lumbered through damp birch and bracken fern last August until I had to crash tangled brush to reach the bank of a favorite, tight, trout stream where I confronted a deep layer of muck between myself and the cold, clear flow where I wanted to be. I fly fish without waders mostly, so stepping through muck would give the leeches that live there the opportunity to attack my legs and feet. Fortunately, three logs crossed over the bank, so I stepped up on the highest and balanced over the muck above the water when my right foot slipped, I wind-milled and dumped on my side, hard, breaking my favorite, handmade rod in three pieces and leaving a grand contusion on my arse that took a month to heal.

THE AGE WE SEASON

It's moments like these that force me to concede that many facets of my active life are going this way. Despite my contrary fantasies, all evidence points to my physical decline: knee reconstruction and both rotator cuffs repaired; baldness, chubbiness. I look in the mirror and think, "How the hell did this happen?" and yearn for the magic of a wild and athletic youth that only my inconsistent memory and a few photographs have captured.

Denial is a comforting liar, but lately I've tried to accept that my turn will eventually come, just as I watched my father and my long time fishing partner, George, age past their abilities to fish. I can still feel the muggy Fathers' Day evening years ago during the Brown Drake hatch on our favorite river. My father and I waded upstream together into the dark toward a sharp bend clogged with branches and the trunks of downed trees. The light faded and the fishing heated up. It was pitch dark by the time we were to cross the tangles, but as I stepped over the first log, Dad stopped. "You go ahead," he said, and I realized this was the ironic, bitter-sweet moment when the son would out-fish the father. Just above the tangles, a deep, flat-water bend pulled away from the bank, where the largest fish fed. I was half-proud and half-sad as I caught larger and larger trout, bringing them downstream to show him. He would not fish this water again, and passed away from pancreatic cancer several years later.

I also can envision the day George could no longer fish the tight stream where we had spent twenty or so seasons taking turns casting. Toward the end, I was his caretaker, holding his hand to help him into the river, over logs and through heavy currents. That day there was a slight breeze as he teetered through the stream, back casting repeatedly into the tag alders until he accepted his final moments on that stretch of water. He would never return. George took trips to Montana where he cast from a chair, but passed away shortly after my last visit to him. He had been silent all night, then looked up and spoke his final words to me, "Have you been fishing?"

THE AGE WE SEASON

There is a young crew of fishermen in my community now, and I see some of them passing through the phases I did in my teens through my thirties, in which my ego and the incessant pursuit of big fish and photos of big fish melded into stories that had to be shared with other fishermen to bring closure to the catch, presenting to others the evidence that I should be worthy of high status in the fraternity of fishermen. I see them and hear them wax philosophically about the river and the fly, as they should, but some more vociferously than others.

That desire to impress, the counting of fish, the measuring of inches and pounds and the collection of photographs for others to admire, are all functions of the lower brain, where lust resides and where I lived most of my youth. Night fishing, for example, is lower brained. I called it an Id-man activity. It feels dangerous, and half the thrill were moments when raccoons fought on branches above my head, bats caught my fly, beavers suddenly splashed their tails like watermelons from ten story buildings or deer busted out of the brush,

MEDITATIONS ON THE FLY

snorting. To me, though, it was unsophisticated, simply locating promising runs and holes, dragging big mouse, moth and zoo cougar patterns through the current in pursuit of enormous, aggressive, nocturnal brown trout that attacked with every tooth. I fished like this for decades, deep into the night and most often alone. I have photos. It was a primal experience and I fed on it.

Then, fifteen or so years ago, during the peak night hatch of the summer, the Hex hatch, when all the big fish feed, I discovered a half dozen cars by a stretch of stream where in youth I would rarely see anyone. Young guys were on walkie-talkies jogging to the river, trying to stake out the best water. My heart sank, I turned around and drove home, having to accept the times had changed, and so had I.

I am over forty-five years a fly fisherman, now pushing sixty, and in the final phase of the fisherman's philosophy, however long I may last. If my legs hold out, hopefully and with luck, twenty-five or more years. Though I still could, I rarely fish the hex hatch, preferring solitude, and haven't gone out dragging mouse patterns for years.

Now I spend more time in the patient, cerebral zones of my mind, past desire and into a slow, silent appreciation of the glorious, cold water environments that support brook trout I catch on hand-tied dry flies during the day. I think, who knows how many more generations will experience this.

Sometimes after hours of immersion, I stop fishing and find myself standing for long times watching waxwings catch mayflies, identifying species of butterflies or standing still long enough for deer to pass without noticing me.

Emerson in his journals sketched an enormous eyeball atop a body, the "transparent eyeball" that became an integral image in his essay, "Nature." He describes moments like these in which "... all mean egotism vanishes. I become a transparent eye-ball; I am nothing; I see all..."

I had my first fishing dream of the winter last night. I was alone, casting sensuously into a swirling

MEDITATIONS ON THE FLY

current. Such visions, such ethereal moments. They come to me more often now.

Emerson's transparent eyeball

THE VOELKER'S POND ESSAYS

INTRODUCTION

THE VOELKER'S POND ESSAYS

INTRODUCTION

I met John Voelker when I was fifteen years old, near the end of a trip that began when my father and I loaded his Scout II with fly casting and camping gear and began a week-long expedition north from our home in Petoskey, across the Straits of Mackinac through the Upper Peninsula, west, along the route Hemingway's character Nick Adams takes by train to Seney, Michigan, in the famous short story, "Big Two Hearted River." In the story, Nick hikes past the town and the burned-out landscape into the lush countryside to recover from an unspoken wound, and catches trout with every cast using live grasshoppers he'd caught in the cool of the morning, until he hooks, battles, and snaps off the big one at the brim of a swamp, a dangerous swamp he would have to leave for another time.

INTRODUCTION

We, however, drove on a dusty road, were sunburned in August heat, fished all day while getting peppered by deer flies, and caught nothing. Later on in the trip we fished the Two Hearted, and other streams, but my father's final destination, and the true reason for the pilgrimage, lay farther north, past the territory where Hemingway traveled in life, past where Nick Adams travels in fiction, beyond the great boggy flats to the rugged, glacier-worn northern rim of the Upper Peninsula, the land we call Traver Country. There we would meet John Voelker.

To avid readers of 1950's best-sellers and to classic film buffs, Robert Traver, the author, may need no introduction, but others may not know his real name, John Voelker, the man Charles Kuralt befriended after profiling him for his CBS News, *On the Road* series, and who in the end Kuralt said was "the closest thing to a great man [he] ever met."

If you haven't read John Voelker's essays, you may never hear so eloquently how true fishermen

THE VOELKER'S POND ESSAYS

enter the world of trout, and why a person ought to do so. There is no machismo or conquest with Voelker. There are few considerations of size and weight, relative to fish or fly. He does not tell where to fish or how to get there or where to stay. What you'll find is a fair amount of self-deprecating humor, deft descriptions of flubbed-up casts and other failures turned to happiness, so that losing a fly while balancing through a bog leads to meeting a friend on the other side. For Voelker, fishing is a joyous pursuit full of humor, humility, and friendships, and other ingredients necessary for approaching "trout wisdom."

Charles Kuralt & John Voelker

INTRODUCTION

Born a bartender's son in 1903 in Ishpeming, on the northern rim of Michigan's Upper Peninsula, Voelker somehow made his way from this most remote and distant region of the state, 500 or so miles south to Ann Arbor where at first he nearly flunked out, then in the end earned a University of Michigan law degree. There he met and afterward married Grace Taylor from Oak Park, Hemingway's hometown, and took a position with a large firm in Chicago. But he could not stand the oppressive, entry-level job or urban life, and soon returned to the U.P. where he was elected district attorney, and where he began writing under the name Robert Traver. Later on, he was elevated to the Michigan Supreme Court before leaping to fame with the success of his best seller, *Anatomy of a Murder*, a novel that soon after was turned into an Academy Award winning film directed by Otto Preminger and starring Jimmy Stewart, Lee Remick, and George C. Scott.

THE VOELKER'S POND ESSAYS

Voelker with Otto Preminger & John Welch (who played the judge in *Anatomy of a Murder*)

Impressive as they are, his political, legal, and literary successes did not immortalize Voelker in the world of fly-fishing; rather, he was immortalized by his willingness to abandon them. At the height of his power, of fame as an author and of influence in the highest court in Michigan, he chose to "flee the baying hounds of success" by stepping down, returning to his simple home in the rugged Upper Peninsula and devoting the rest of his life to his passions: fishing from spring to fall and writing about fishing all winter, a routine that

INTRODUCTION

produced such classics as *Trout Madness, Anatomy of a Fisherman,* and *Trout Magic.*

He became ritualistic — more and more, it seems, as the years went on, picking up his mail in the mornings, meeting friends at the Rainbow Bar in Ishpeming, driving over 20 miles of dirt road to avoid one mile of pavement on his way to fish camp, fishing until the five o'clock cabin break for cocktails and cribbage. But all the while, in mind and in motion, alone or with his closest friends, he pursued the shy, native brook trout that haunt the vast waterways of the Escanaba River basin, and especially — particularly — the "mermaids" in a remote stretch of spring — fed water he owned, where my father and I would join him.

At times he and his friends called the place "Frenchman's Creek" ("for that is not its name," he wrote) or "Frenchman's," "Frenchman's Pond," "Uncle Tom's," "Uncle's" or "fish camp," and he wrote lovingly of its inhabitants' feminine dispositions. He could catch trout there only when they were, as he put it, "in the mood."

THE VOELKER'S POND ESSAYS

Learning to fly-fish with me was one of my father's most profound gifts, more than he would know, but equally, so was this pilgrimage to meet a man who had achieved the heights of success and was willing to chuck all social expectation with a confident grin, who was unafraid to live on his own terms, and who chose to spend his time simply and humbly, among friends, fishing the vast waterways in the landscape that he loved.

Voelker at the bar with friends

INTRODUCTION

Voelker's fishing notes, July 15, 1976, mentioning the author's visit

THE ROAD IN

We met him in the parking lot, shook hands, and he smiled right away, calling me "Seamus" though that is not my name, and I liked him immediately. Tall with big hands and a weathered happy face, he was dressed in khaki pants and shirt with a cigar sticking out of the pocket, worn leather boots and a round, weather-worn hat with a small brim. "Well," he said then, and turned to his fish car. My father and I piled into our Scout and followed him out of town at ten miles under the speed limit and slower still when we hit dirt roads, then down to a trot on the two-tracks, snailing along for miles, watching the back of his white Jeep, brake lights on more than off. I still remember the tension between my desire to show respect and my adolescent need to get somewhere. Finally frustrated enough with his opossum's pace I said, "Where's he going?" I was certain we'd turned at one time or another to every point on the compass. I looked to my father, who shrugged.

Then he stopped. I thought finally we had arrived at a trail to a fishing hole, but his door did not open. Instead, an arm extended out of his window, then a finger pointed at something on the ground that we could not make out until we pulled ahead and craned our necks to see a nest of white orchids, delicate, cupped like children's hands, nearly hidden by undergrowth a foot or two off the beaten track. We admired them as he got out with a pair of snippets and clipped one. There was a pause, then my dad asked, "Aren't those protected?"

"Well," he said, "from time to time I have to bend the statute, sir," and he placed the flower in a bucket of water, then hopped back in the Jeep.

THE VOELKER'S POND ESSAYS

Ten minutes later he came to a complete stop again and without a word or glance toward us, he reached into the back of his fish car, retrieved a white plastic bucket, turned and sauntered into the woods. We piled out and waited, wondering what he was up to until he returned with a pair of white shelf-fungus. He said they were edible and grew on dead aspen, but they looked like old boot toes to me, and now I suspect the harvest was part theater, but I was quick to want to please the master.

Voelker's fish car

As we started up again, I searched above the scrub pines for the tops of poplars and within 50

79

yards, deep in the brush I spied the top of a thick, dead aspen and, tracing down toward its trunk, spotted a mound of mushrooms. I marked the tree and called out, "Stop!", frightening my father, and I leaped out through the brambles, returning with my arms heavy with musty mushrooms. I handed them over to Mr. Voelker, who thanked me, a bit undone I think by my performance.

"How did you see those?" my father asked, and I beamed the rest of the way in.

A little later, the judge repeated the orchid trick with his clippers and some wild roses.

Voelker clipping flowers

THE VOELKER'S POND ESSAYS

After an hour or more of four-wheel sauntering, our attention spans sputtering, we followed him off a sandy road onto a lesser worn dirt two-track that descended through second growth pines and over an enormous glacial rock that required slow going, tilting us sideways, then dropping us down a gully and through a small, muddy stream, then up again into some tall birch and aspen and into a tight canopy of maples, where we read a hand-painted sign, "Warning: Bridge Out." A few old fenders, mufflers, and car parts were strewn about there, by way of discouraging the uninvited. We followed, until we came to a thick cable across the road, latched with an old German key lock the size of a woodcutter's fist. He dropped the cable and waved us on, past another sign that read brazenly, "Home of the Upper Peninsula Cribbage Champion," then through an ancient stand of red pines canopied above us, the car having to bump and weave around enormous trunks on a soft matting of needles and over roots round as my thighs. We soon emerged to a sandier section and a more open, flat plain

THE ROAD IN

with aspen and bracken fern, some No Trespassing signs. Then suddenly, from where I was sitting, his Jeep appeared to fall headlong into hole.

The road dropped out from under us also, so steeply that I had to put my hand on the dashboard, but in seconds we were stopped on a flat, gray glacial rock. I stepped out and stretched. On my left, a rough-hewn cabin not much longer than our car, a picnic table, and oddities like horseshoes and telephone insulators, a pair of wooden minstrels. On my right, the sloping rock and lichen path down to the dark water of Frenchman's pond.

THE POND

Frenchman's is an ice-cold backwater created by a series of active beaver dams that have stood for well over 50 years, maybe 100. Its water is relatively shallow and seeps up from a mosquito rich cedar swamp, filtered clean through deep, easily disturbed silt beds that rest on glacier-raked bedrock, billions of years old. The surrounding landscape was formed by the final recession, ten thousand years ago, of an ice field so thick and vast it shaped the entire Midwest, depositing sand and rich soils in vast moraines, carving out the Great Lakes and leaving behind Lake Superior, only a few miles north.

THE POND

From deep in bedrock, water seeps up in springs where trout congregate in the evening and early morning, and on most overcast days. Otherwise they seek the cover of fallen trees, sunken casting stations, weed beds, and undercut banks. But then again, they may decide to feed actively in shallow water on a sunny day, against all sense, or hide for days, leaving fishermen to believe the water is barren.

Voelker called it Frenchman's, "for that is not its name." Like all great fishermen, he would never kiss and tell on a trout stream, but neither could he have predicted how rapidly the outside world would expand into his own. In the late '50s, when he began writing about the pond, the Upper Peninsula was only accessible from the Lower Peninsula by ferry. It wasn't until the completion of the Mackinac bridge, the "fatal artery," that allowed downstaters to travel at highway speeds into Traver Country.

When I visited in the mid 1976 his cabin was remote, but I doubt he could have imagined then how quickly the world would impinge. I wonder if he would have named it at all. Still, Frenchman's never was open for business.

Its beauty is moody, often muted, mercurial, and intimate, and it defies definition: at high water, it is a creek with a pond's vegetation and a tedious but distinct current. At low water, it is a still, cold-water pond more difficult to fish, more confined. It requires you to slow down, to settle into its own rhythms, yet it makes no promises, except that you earn your keep; it does not impress itself upon you with raging currents or wide sweeping bends, but lulls you into noticing the smallest, most remarkable things: a spider's web, a ringlet of water, a cedar waxwing feeding on something too small for you to see.

Walking the shoreline of Frenchman's Pond is like balancing across a floating field of trapdoors. The ground is pitted and knolled with old stumps hidden in the grass, and clumped with roots, and troughed by ancient beaver runs, and pocked by muskrat holes. There are low, dark inlets that

THE POND

might provide you hard ground to stand on, or you might be in muck three feet deep. Sometimes you set a foot down certain it will hold you, only to find what looked like grass was a vegetable veneer. As you cast, here and there, a lone branch from a low shrub tricks you and snaps off your fly, or restricts you to roll-casts that rarely, and at best barely stretch far enough to reach the few rising trout you see.

You might circumnavigate the entire pond only to find the vibration of your bumbling footwork has sent the trout down or driven them back to the other side. Or it could be that whatever invisible insect they have keyed in on has stopped hatching where you are, and started where they are. Once, while the rest of the pond remained glassy and still, I witnessed a hatch and feeding fish in an area maybe ten feet in diameter, and nowhere else on the entire pond, a column of mayflies performing their vertical dance, fluttering up, floating down, fluttering up again above the concentric, liquid ringlets of feeding trout, and all of this beyond the reach of my longest cast.

Wading across is impossible, and wading in general is dangerous, since stepping past the bank might mean oozing waist deep into jet-black, boot-sucking muck. Either way, stuck or not, the richest silt releases methane bubbles that percolate up your legs in a witch's stench, leaving you relieved you don't smoke, and certain that even if you somehow survive, a week's worth of tomato baths may not gain you acceptance again in the civilized world. And yet, I wade now and again, probing, prodding, negotiating my own way through.

THE CABIN

THE CABIN

He could have hired architects to erect a monumental home on some western river, or on a high bank over the Escanaba or Lake Superior, but instead he and his friends found the only solid, flat slab of ground on Frenchman's and built a cedar and pine cabin, shaped like a miniature barn, barely big enough for four people, cramped with five, tucked between the hemlocks at the bottom of a steep bank, only a stone's throw from the pond.

Outside they built a brick stove, a table opposite the cabin door, a storage shed and a rail fence leading to the privy, a sign marking the way, warning: "Bare Area." They never bothered to build walls or a roof, just a plywood box with a hole under a toilet seat and an empty coffee can for the paper. There is no running water or electricity at Frenchman's.

Beside the cabin, they chained a cooler to a tree behind an old picnic table, and over the years added knickknacks and oddities to the trees and shelves along the cabin: license plates and wood-carved minstrels, old glass insulators from telephone poles, a thermometer and such.

Facing the cabin, an old bell still hangs above the door. I have never pulled its rope, but imagine its tone echoing down the pond to ring in the fishermen for four o'clock cocktails, the fishing reports, and friendly wagering.

Inside, the cabin is three paces wide and six deep with sliding glass windows on three sides and a woodstove on the fourth. Memorabilia adorn most shelves and wall space, harkening themes from the old man's writings, his life and works. Tacked to the wall: an old advertisement for Griffin reels with the image of a curvaceous mermaid, taunting, "You'll never catch me without a Griffin Reel;" an original cover of *Trout Magic*; a republished cover of *Trout Madness*; a faded copy of his "Testament to a Fisherman." Also, the echoes of male yearnings: an oil painting of a woman, naked from the waist up, postcards, one from France of two nudes in soft light, and on a shelf, a glass that reads, CAUTION: CONTENTS OF THIS GLASS MAY LEAD TO INTERCOURSE. Handwritten and painted greeting cards, faded photos of friends and high up, a line of spent bourbon bottles. The cribbage board, candles and cards rest on a custom table with drink shelves built into the legs. Along the south wall, farthest from the pond, an old green couch that folds out to a bed (I didn't discover this for years).

 For years I held a reverence for the memorabilia inside the cabin, and snooped, but to find a spoon or a match. But this year as his family began cleaning and rearranging the cabin, I confess I snooped one night after fishing, alone. There is a hanging shelf above with blankets and a comforter I'd donated years before. I was taking the blanket down when

THE CABIN

I noticed a box full of heavy papers that with a glance I found were maps.

My father and I used to keep plat maps of all the counties where we hunted and fished, so we could study the boundaries between state and private land. We always noted the good grouse hunting or the access roads to rivers. A skull and crossbones where the going is too rough, an exclamation point, or the number of grouse flushes. I thought, could it be that I have found the fountain of knowledge from the High Priest of Secrecy; the master woodsman who vowed never to kiss and tell on a trout stream? I pulled down the box to find over 20 maps of Baraga and Marquette counties and flipped through them one by one like mad, searching for a single mark, a green penmark, a comment in the margins, anything to indicate success or failure.

What I found were the pages of pristine maps, and the truest lesson of Traver's legacy: Go, young man, and find it for yourself.

THE VOELKER'S POND ESSAYS

FISHING, WISHING, AND WATCHING

My father and the judge made conversation by the cabin while I walked down to the water where a short dock protruded from thick bramble bushes that lined the entire rim of the pond. I stepped out to the end and squatting down, was struck by the illusion of depth created by auburn water, rich with tannin, over black silt. From farther back it could have been 10 or 20 feet deep, but up close, at most, the water looked only three or four and most of it appeared to be a foot or less. I stuck a stick into the bottom, and it disappeared into the silt without hitting firm ground. Then I stood up, and

FISHING, WISHING, AND WATCHING

for some time watched the long draw of upstream water while the men chatted and unpacked gear. I did not see rising trout and I felt poorly about my prospects. Still, I was moved to be in so remote and rugged a landscape, the guest of a famous, gracious man who placed fishing above all things, and I remember a calm comfort, gratitude, and a sense of belonging that would one day call me back.

To my left, downstream, a trail led through tall hemlocks and pines over moss-covered bedrock to the narrow neck of the hourglass pond where a wooden bridge spanned the creek, complete with church pews, one facing upstream, the other down, and staggered, so that fishermen sitting across from each other could watch the water and not each other. Here, he had said, was a place for "trout devotionals." A wrought-iron weather vane shaped like a fish was raised like a steeple between the pews. I peered over the side, hoping to spot a fish or two, but didn't, and so sat down while a family of chipmunks skittered to my feet with brazen expectation, having been fed there so frequently.

Milk crates were used for casting stations.

"Well," my father called to me through the pines, "You fishing?"

I hopped up and hiked back to the Scout, rigged up my rod and strapped into my oversized rubber waders.

"I'll take the lad," the judge said, dutifully. Following him over the bridge, I then stumbled behind his steady gait along planks that spanned unevenly the muck and grassy ground to a casting station made of wooden crates about midway up the main pond. My father watched us from the dock with a camera.

"Be my guest, my boy," the Judge said with a swagger and a wave toward the pond.

I was an adequate fisherman on rivers with wet flies because I knew how to present a muddler minnow downstream — a skill that did not necessarily require casting. I'd learned I could take a handful of line and pitch it upstream above a pool, letting it sink, then mend line like crazy into the current, getting a streamer deep down and across until I thought it would be in front of a decent fish — then I'd quickly strip it across the pool. It was ugly but effective.

Here, though, on Frenchman's with the Master at my side, I felt whoozie, knowing I had nothing in my bag of tricks to help me. But I tried.

First, with eyes focused on the water I stripped line out of my reel straight into the brambles, snagging up a rat's nest before I could even begin a cast. Apologizing, I cleared the knots, holding excess line in my left hand. Now focusing again on a dark spot of water 20 feet out, I set myself like a quarterback, released the slack line in my hand and whipped a back cast up high into the one shrub behind us, violating the first rule of the forward cast, which is first to check on the back cast.

Now I was breathing embarrassment, defeat and shame, hobbling through the brush to free my fly from top branches, only to discover my line had been dragging behind me all the way, tangling like silly string in the brambles.

THE VOELKER'S POND ESSAYS

I struggled back to him, finally reassembled, and he looked down at me with a wry smile. "You might want to work on the roll cast, my boy," he said, and stepped up, stripping line from his reel and singing it once through the guides of his old cane rod into the pond. Then, with a slow back and upward motion he lifted the line briefly toward himself and slightly off the water until it bowed just behind the rod tip, and in one fluid motion he put on forward pressure, accelerating the line into a loop, lifting the entire length of line, leader, tippet and fly with a graceful flip, 15 feet out, then again, looping line nearly halfway across the pond. I thought of an old sailor I'd seen in Harbor Springs who tied a bowline one-handed, with a single flip of the arm, a trick I never mastered, or a crusty old cowboy who could loop your boot while riding, whistling "Dixie" too. Within three casts he was landing a trout.

He released the troutling and stepped aside, smiled, then wandered up to another station while I set about trying to imitate his fluid motions by piling line into the water, no doubt terrorizing trout for a full half hour, until at last I caught my shirtsleeve, then nearly pierced my nose with a number four Muddler Minnow. With that I decided nonchalantly to excuse myself, hobbling back to the bridge where I settled in, feeding the chipmunks and watching the judge roll out his line.

My father had been out of sight downstream at the large beaver dam all morning. Just after midday he met me on the bridge and claimed to have caught a few small trout that he released, but nothing more. I described my roll-casting fiasco, and he sat with me for a while, then he headed toward the truck to get out of his waders.

Watching the judge fish, I thought in my juvenile way that he might have offered me more instruction. But that was the way of these men, to show me once or twice and leave me alone to face my inadequacies and inaccuracies. Failure is good. It teaches.

I'm not sure how much it mattered to them if I persevered in this or other matters. In fishing, as in life, I would be learning alone how to be rejected, to fail and fail again, so that in the end, whether intended or not, I might discover a proper perspective, a set of priorities, and here anyway, let the landscape be the teacher.

And so, Frenchman's teaches that joy is in the pursuit as much as the catching, or you'll find certain misery much of the time; joy is in the opportunity, so that you'll not forget gratitude; and in the failures, since we learn the same lessons over and over — how to observe, to approach, to find fluidity of movement that communicates with the living world.

Still, I wished I'd caught a fish.

COCKTAILS AND CRIBBAGE WITH MEN

THE VOELKER'S POND ESSAYS

COCKTAILS AND CRIBBAGE WITH THE MEN

That day, sitting on the bridge watching him, I didn't know who he was, not really. I understood he was an important man, but I hadn't read his books yet. Still, something struck me deeply about him. I never got to know my own grandfather, but while writing this book I found from my mother that the judge and he had a grand old time one summer night in my backyard, drinking together into the wee hours. My mother was a good friend to Voelker's wife, Grace, and I wondered what the women endured with these men.

But after an hour or so, his casts could not evoke another rise, he ambled back to me at the

COCKTAILS AND CRIBBAGE WITH THE MEN

bridge and sat down. I could not think of a thing to say, so we sat for a few minutes of silence on the pews. My father soon joined us and we all sat silently for some time suspended over the glassy pond, the wilderness on one side, the cabin on the other.

Then at once, we all breathed out loud, stood up and shuffled over to the cabin. There were sandwiches and sodas for me in the cooler outside, but like a boy at a tavern door with a message for his father, I did not know whether I was welcome to enter, and neither man seemed interested in me. The two had already made sandwiches and the judge mixed up his legendary old-fashioneds in tin cups.

"Well, sir," I heard the judge say, "would you like a friendly wager and a chance at the title?"

Serious men deep in competition do not typically request the company of long-haired fifteen year olds, but having nowhere else to go, I crept into the cabin with the notion that perhaps I'd be included. Neither man suggested I leave, so I watched my father somehow win the first round of cribbage, relieving the judge of a prized quarter, handed over to him by a much surprised and dissatisfied Upper Peninsula Cribbage Champion, who in turn suggested another game and another wager, five dollars. A friendly tension even a vacant teenager could detect suddenly seeped through the cabin, making it seem much smaller, so not comprehending cribbage or half their witticisms and allusions anyway, I slipped outside and walked up on the high bank overlooking the pond, sitting by myself for a long time, thinking. Later, my father would tell me the old man skunked him twice in a row, taking ten bucks with a grin and an "I thank you, sir."

By then, the day was spent, the fishing was over and we followed the judge out, somehow arriving on pavement in a manner of minutes, when it had taken hours on the way in.

COCKTAILS AND CRIBBAGE WITH THE MEN

Voelker, cocktail in hand, in his cabin

THE VOELKER'S POND ESSAYS

HIS JUSTICES' FLIES

I'm fifty-seven, with few vices left, and I envy no one. I do, however, covet other men's fly collections, when they surpass my own.

It is a weakness compounded by my own compulsion to give away the flies I've spent the winter tying, to friends, even to strangers at times, just for the simple joy of believing their fishing will be improved by my inventions. So imagine my eyes when Voelker's grandson, Adam, first unveiled the vast array of flies he'd inherited: piles of them, a veritable history lesson in the evolution of the fly from the 1930's to the present, mostly tied by Voelker's friends — and none tied by Voelker himself.

"Far from being able to tie a fly, I am barely able to unzip one," he wrote.

Adam had stepped to a closet in his living room and handled a large crate, unpacking box after box, some handmade out of plastic pill containers and such, as I recall the Judge having when I first met him (he had a box on which he'd written: "WARNING: This box contains the world's deadliest flies"), some in pricey Wheatley boxes (most of which, Adam told me, were gifts), most of them curiously unorganized on the insides. Dry flies were mixed with wet, large and small, duns, emergers, streamers, no-hackles, bushy hackles in every color and combination, some elegant, some sloppy, some clearly having caught their share of fish. I picked through them, speechless.

Then Adam said, "Oh," and stood up, stepping back to the closet, returning with his grandfather's vest and pulling out something silvery cupped in his hand. He set it on the counter: an old 1960's film container, tin, with a screw-on lid, dented and scuffed. He unscrewed the top and spilled out about two dozen flies: mini-streamers and size 28 midge and larvae flies. With a pencil tip, he pushed the tiniest of them aside. "This one," he said, pointing to a yellow dot on a wire hook smaller than a pencil tip, "is supposed to be the egg sack off a henspinner." He paused a moment, then said, "These were in my grandfather's breast pocket when he died."

GIZMOS IN THE PURSUIT

THE VOELKER'S POND ESSAYS

GIZMOS IN THE PURSUIT

In the cases of John Voelker and his friends, *Trout Madness* was the mother of invention. The brook trout in his pond and adjacent waterways eluded them so frequently, they set their minds constantly on ways to improve their pursuits, including building casting stations and boardwalks, but also inventing what we now find in pricey catalogs as "float tubes." Theirs were tractor inner tubes with hand-tied diaper slings that would let a man drift over water too deep for waders.

And in the case of the infamous Dancing Fly, if we are to take the story seriously, his friends learned to stand on opposite banks of the pond with their lines tied together and a fly on a dropper between them, pulling it back and forth to make it dance. And though they had a mind to do it, they fell short of fishing from balloons.

But there were other tricks. For quick extraction from one fishing hole and insertion in the next, rather than breaking down all the equipment and having to re-rig it at the next site on the river, the judge would break the rod down only, with the line and fly still rigged, laying it carefully on a towel, rolling it up and wrapping it with pipe cleaners. That way when he arrived, it was a matter of seconds and he was on the river, fly already attached.

To me, because of its novelty, one of the niftiest inventions was sitting on the table when Adam showed us his grandfather's deep collection of flies. There was first a homemade clip-on magnifying glass that had a Paul Young clipper and tweezer, but the novelty was this odd looking wooden clothespin with a spring on it, an item Adam thinks his grandfather may have invented himself.

It was a tool, I was told, for tying the essential but difficult knot, the "blood knot," used when a fisherman needs to link two uneven sizes of tippet or leader together. It's a painful knot to learn, requiring the tier first to hold the two unequal ends of the leader together in an "X" — the thicker leader that is already attached to the line, and the new, thinner, leader or tippet he hopes to attach. He must then take one end at a time — in this case, the thinner line — twisting it four or five times around the thicker line and bringing it back to the original point of contact and through where the two pieces met originally to form the "X." He must hold it there without losing his grip as he then turns the thicker end an equal number of times over the thinner line, using one hand, since the other is busy, bringing that end back so that now both ends have passed through the hole that was formed once the second line began twisting. Most of the time failure occurs at this point, when one or both of the ends slip out and the whole mess untangles. When tied successfully, however, the knot is super strong and can be clipped smooth, so if by accident the fisherman casts poorly, the hook does not hang on his own leader.

So here is what the good judge figured out. He took a common clothespin and fit a flat piece of metal he'd designed under one of the forward pin springs so it was locked down in front, with a piece like a tail pointing toward the back of the clothespin. This tail was thin enough to slide inside a small tight spring. He inserted the spring, then locked it down near the pincher end of the clothespin using wood putty. After the putty dried, he rolled up a piece of scratch paper, sticking it under the spring, so the spring arced, opening up its coils slightly.

Now, when it came time to tie a blood knot, he could place his rod on his lap and clip the clothespin to his rod, then lay each piece of leader and tippet into the grooves of the spring. The spring held them nicely parallel and snugly so both his hands were free. He could then tie each half of the knot without ever worrying about letting go or it slipping out of his hands. He'd snug up the wraps, give a little pull on the leader and tippet, and both would pop out of the spring; the knot would tighten and be ready for trimming.

I wish I could have seen him whip up a knot like that beside some other poor sap trying to do the same, a twinkle in his eye, even if that poor sap had been me.

EQUIPMENT

EQUIPMENT

According to Adam, after his grandfather passed away, some time went by before he could get back to Ishpeming, but when he did he discovered much of the fishing gear he would eventually inherit spread out throughout the house. In one room he found several of his grandfather's rods in a corner loosely bundled in a large wicker basket. About four or five of them were fully assembled, others not, among them, some of his grandfather's favorites. Two rods were hanging crisscrossed above the mirror in the bedroom. In the basement he found a number of empty rod tubes, some corresponding with rods upstairs, some not, most of them with lost caps and others containing extra tips but no matching rods. Reels and line and miscellaneous tools that had not been gifted away were mostly boxed up. His grandmother had neatened up most of his flies and placed them in a large cardboard box. There was no way to take an inventory. Before Adam was able to take possession of the collection, there may have been a bit of a grab bag going on among visitors, but who could say.

Of course, Adam had inherited a gold mine of memorabilia, one that would arouse his interest in cane rods, their histories and restoration, and that would lead him to become a collector, connoisseur, and an authority on the evolution of American cane rods.

His grandfather knew a fine piece of split bamboo from a buggy whip. Most of the rods Adam inherited were hand built by the best craftsmen of the day and had become as much a part of the lore of his grandfather's yarns as the pond and his beloved fish car.

THE VOELKER'S POND ESSAYS

I sat with Adam in his kitchen, looking over the craftsmanship of a genuine Thomas rod built in 1928. It came with two tips personally restored by the legendary Paul Young in 1945. This was the same rod mentioned in *Trout Magic* where Voelker writes, "I still have several rods made by Paul [Young] himself (now prized collectors' items) including one real oldie Paul used himself, a weepy old Thomas that used to make me feel like Nijinsky himself when I get waving it with a full head of line."

Next to this rod, Adam had set out a Kushner rod, the very Kushner in the essay, "Morris the Rod Maker." Next to that, another Paul Young designed to be fished on the Au Sable from one of the classic, narrow, flat-bottomed Au Sable River boats. It's a long, beefy rod with a special thumb impression, to give power through the butt of the rod rather than the midsection, allowing a more comfortable cast from a sitting position. For those who have a copy of *Anatomy of a Fisherman*, you can see this rod resting against a tree if you look

EQUIPMENT

closely at the shot of Voelker sitting in the rain. Other rods were dispersed to friends before his death, and one, an Orvis Limestone Special, along with a favorite sweater and an old tin cup, rests in the care of the Fly Fishing Hall of Fame.

Through the 1980s and '90s the technology of fly rod design blossomed, and occasionally, especially when fishing the big water on the Escanaba or when he encountered a blustery day, Voelker would set aside his willowy cane rods and pull out a meatier fiberglass model, or one particular graphite rod built in the 1970s. They were powerful tools, no doubt, but he claimed, unlike his old bamboo, they did not have "soul." Toward the end, as his powers waned, the judge was seen on Frenchman's with his favorite cane rods, rolling out fine tippets and flies, more often sitting down on a crate or a chair than standing.

Ever since hearing these stories, one question has remained with me, mostly because it reminded me of my own equipment foibles. Why did the judge, knowing the value of his equipment, treat it all so nonchalantly, leaving them in corners still assembled when they should have been broken down; sticking flies in the cork butts rather than on hook eyes; losing caps to rod cases and misplacing matching parts?

Perhaps it was a sentiment, or rather, an accident of personality I may share with him. He no doubt appreciated a lovely rod — as do I — especially those handcrafted beauties offered to him by friends. But I think it's clear that to a man in love with the woods, rods, reels, flies — they are only tools — beautiful tools, no doubt, but only tools.

Nowhere in his Testament of a Fisherman, his most compressed and often quoted expression on fishing, does he mention the sensuous feel of a rod or reel, the elegance of a perfect cast, or the power a well-made rod can wave. He never mentions the clock like precision or capacities or the thrill of line whining out of a Hardy reel at the behest of a granddaddy trout. These may have all been sweet possessions and sweet pleasures, but they had little to do with love. "I fish because I love to," he said.

EQUIPMENT

He loved the trout and the environs where they are found. He loved the peace and solitude these environs offered him. Equipment — rods, reels, lines, they were only possessions — tippets, and flies coveted no doubt by some men — brandished with pride by others — but to him, I think they were merely a means for communicating with the environs he loved, and for that, in the end, no tools are necessary.

I think above all, he most loved the blessed opportunity to fish, and if not to fish, to sit on a church pew in the presence of water — these things above all the baubles men worship in this world. "Only when I can no longer cast to one of my beauties will I consider letting go," he said. And though now he is gone, he leaves this lesson for those who are listening.

THE VOELKER'S POND ESSAYS

Voelker with his friend, Judge Carroll Rustin, "The Old Fox"

A WITNESS TO THE DANCING FLY

A WITNESS TO THE DANCING FLY

In the waning hours of the afternoon I wandered upstream on the cabin side of the pond along Voelker's trail, now moss-covered and lush, but still imprinted in the soft earth. It is always cooler under the hemlocks and cedars, shaded and fragrant. Past the second dam the trail faded, overgrown with lush foliage, swamp grasses and thistles, wildflowers and lichens. Dense, mature hemlocks and cedars lined the second pond on the cabin side where the bank falls steeply to the water, but on the far side drowned hardwoods line the shore, some of them having toppled into the water, others hollowed out over the years, their trunks pocked by woodpeckers.

The last fishable pond upstream was like this. Half submerged maples and aspens lay one over another, providing ample cover for wary trout as well as wood ducks, and good hunting for herons, raccoons, and otters, and making for tricky fishing, their branches both above and below the surface waiting to snatch a fly. Certainly the largest trout lurked far back in the deepest cover, where even a wizard could not cast a line.

It had been a rare and sensuous afternoon in the middle of May, a day devoid of human sounds, windless and warm, easing into evening. A hatch was inevitable, tangible and anticipated in the scented, humid air. By the beginnings of twilight flycatchers and cedar waxwings appeared in the treetops, now and again flipping out from branches to snatch last night's mayflies as they began their airborne mating dance. The day waned into magic time — that window of light when day creatures retreat to night, and night creatures stir to day, and the pond comes alive.

The sun passed over the tree line, casting the pond in pastel half-light while slowly, like an orchestra tuning, a chorus of crickets and cicadas and songbirds, whippoorwills and white-throated sparrows, spring peepers, crows, chickadees and jays swelled to a crescendo. Overhead a hawk circled, and a mink darted across a log into the opposite bank. Then a hatch of tiny caddis and midges and moths came on and the pond slowly percolated with feeding fish. A doe walked the shore across the way, unaware, followed by two fawns, and a great horned owl, its enormous wingspan startling me, swept up onto the top of a hollow tree, and coyotes, yip-yip-yowled and barked into the dark. A grouse drummed in the distance and woodcock made their twittering mating flights overhead. And I was glad to the brink of tears, fallen into a separate, timeless state, so much so that the pond and all its inhabitants breathed a chorus with me that I felt in the belly, in the chest. It settles from the mind to the body, to the actions of the extremities — legs sliding through water, arms testing the length of the cast, then committing, reaching up and across a log or a slow, swirling current, a quick midair mend of line, all unconscious, muscular, free. Immersed in sensuous water, giving flight and direction to the proper length of line, compensating here for breeze and there for the high cedar behind me.

Then, just before full dark, there emerged from the water a rich and magical hatch of the "dancing fly" Voelker describes in *Trout Magic*, an iridescent yellow insect he aptly described as an "animated ball of fur," miniscule, and impossible to match with a fly — so far — because it literally hops on the water, stirring the fish into a frenzy and bringing the pond to a boil. I watched, absorbed, unable to catch another fish but thrilled and finally exhausted as darkness came on, the pond settled down, and I turned to the stars and sighed.

… THE VOELKER'S POND ESSAYS

NATIVE TROUT AND TELEVISION

In his essay, "Size Is Not the Measure," Voelker noted a growing preference fisherman were expressing for larger species of fish, claiming that he had not seen a single photo of a brook trout adorning the pages of outdoor magazines in months, maybe years, and feared that the new obsession with bigger and bigger fish was "inevitably transplanting to our trout waters the whole competitive, strident, screechingly acquisitive world of business."

"Worse yet," he said, "fishermen were sacrificing one of the main rewards and solaces of going fishing at all, namely, that fishing is … the world's only sport that it is fun even to fail at." He finally admitted he was "sad beyond words that fishermen themselves would let one of the world's oldest and loveliest contemplative pastimes turn into a competitive rat race."

The judge wrote this in 1974, judiciously.

Last month, hoping to take a nap, I flipped on an outdoor channel only to see a "fly-fishing competition," in which "professional" fly-fishermen and women drew sections of a Western creek, were given time limits and set out to catch the largest possible fish for prize money, catching, measuring, and tossing back. I couldn't believe what I was watching, except that once again men have proved that anything sacred can be appropriated and packaged.

Only one competitor, a woman, seemed to have a decent attitude throughout, enjoying herself, coming in third or fourth, but having had fun. For the rest, it was testosterone and intensity. After the awards, the camera lit for awhile on a pudgy young man who'd not "won" anything, holding his head in his hands to hide his tears.

I had to laugh because I couldn't reach inside the television and bop the heartsick boy upside the head. Then I sighed and thought how grounding it is to retreat to the pond, where I had inherited the priorities of a wise man, and where the world operates on principles of beauty and where every trout is a gem, not a measurement; where each is cherished for its wildness, and where we take time to note the striking variety of their complexions and color, some of them far lighter and greener, with brighter yellow spotting, while others are nearly all the deepest blue, with haloed, azure rings around radiant maroon moons intermittently spaced along their medial lines. And we notice, as fall approaches, the spawning season, their colors intensify; the larger males taking on orange bellies and hooking jaws, the blues and greens, purples and yellows, white pectoral fins and black lines. I am always amazed that these creatures — so radiant in my hand — can disappear so easily once they slip back underwater. They rival in beauty any fish in the world, freshwater or tropical.

Brown trout, and lake run rainbows no doubt, are the giants of the larger streams, and are thrilling to catch, but they are not native to Traver Country. Only the wild brook trout are indigenous here.

And in this way, they are not only great fun to pursue and fail to catch, but they represent all true inhabitants of the region — inhabitants — not immigrants or residents — but inhabitants whose lives are intertwined with every element of the landscape, the pond in which they live, its temperatures and depths. And they remind us of the other human inhabitants, like Voelker himself, who stayed in his community, who witnessed its changes, heard the old dialects slowly lost to what he called a "bastard form of televese" and the influx of fast food and mass markets and strip malls and a pace of life that has led even fly fishermen to forget that every day is a glorious opportunity, and that there are no bad days on a stream.

THE VOELKER'S POND ESSAYS

No brook trout would have been large enough to win that competition on television. I wonder what the old judge would have said to the fisherman who wept for money and esteem on the banks of that lovely stretch of trout-rich water.

CHANGES AND PERMANENCE

CHANGES AND PERMANENCE

It is a harsh landscape by the pond, come winter, when on average 129 inches of snow will fall. What can creatures eat enduring an ice field like that? And consider the immigrants, also, who made their homesteads there in the 1800's, as did Voelker's family and those in the communities he knew so well.

And as a case in point from the animal world, consider that every county in the Lower Peninsula, and nearly every county in the state has had perennial over populations of deer except Baraga and Marquette counties and the few others on the northern rim by Lake Superior where the landscape resembles the region around the pond. And from those counties nearly all the deer that summer there migrate south in the fall by long-established routes, knowing not to return until spring.

So, in the years that have passed since John Voelker left us, approximately 4,773 inches of snow and Lord knows how much rain has fallen on the fish camp, taking with them the old bridge and pews, toppling into the pond. From a rock ledge above, when the light is right you can see the sunken structure; it has made good fish cover. Several beauties have been landed there. There is some poetic justice.

The old planks that made the boardwalks across the bog have disappeared completely, while casting stations and milk crates, all lichen and moss—covered, have drooped into the boggy ground or slipped half into the pond or rusted or disappeared altogether, so that looking at what remains one can't be sure if the weight of winter snowfall flattened them or some subterranean forces sucked them down.

THE VOELKER'S POND ESSAYS

The closer we look, the more respect we have for the tenacity of every living thing in and on and around the pond. A violent windstorm boasting gales of 80 mph hit the area around the pond this past summer, leveling trees for miles, snapping pines in half like toothpicks, knocking power and water out for people in the nearby townships, and on the pond, nearly crushing the cabin. A 40-foot hemlock fell over the road, straight for the cabin, but caught on the two larger hemlocks beside it, and on the other side large hemlocks were blown over, uprooted completely, but fell away from the cabin, uphill.

And as a testament even to the tenacity of tree life itself, across the narrows where the bridge once stood, a 40-foot hemlock had been uprooted in the storm, leaving beneath it a barren rock face. Though in the end it fell, for 30 years or more, however old it was, it had clung to the face of a billion year old, barren rock and sapped enough nutrients to grow, who knows how. When it fell, all that remained was a sheer face of granite falling straight into the pond.

Anyway, despite the clear-cuttings that have crept closer and closer, and despite whippings by Lake Superior gales, despite summer droughts and blizzards and the heavy swelling waters of spring, the pond remains the same, in shape and size and personality — enigmatic and permanent.

Not long ago, Adam gave me a first edition of *Anatomy of a Fisherman*, the photo-essay hardcover, but my wife, Lisa, had not seen it until recently. In it are several shots of Voelker on his pond, standing exactly as I have, landing one of his largest brookies of that summer in the lower pond, exactly where I stood, landing one of the largest of this summer, my wife Lisa standing by me, camera in hand. It is uncanny ... this pond, this legacy.

THE VOELKER'S POND ESSAYS

The author, fishing Frenchman's

A VIEW INTO THE UPPER PONDS

… THE VOELKER'S POND ESSAYS

A VIEW INTO THE UPPER PONDS

It was late August. A whisper of autumn had passed in the morning air, but now afternoon turned lovely, hot and blue-bright, and the mermaids sought the comforts of cover in the lower ponds, turning up their noses at every cast, no matter how delicately proposed, and no matter what elegant or gaudy fashion of fly landed at their window. Rejected, lulled a bit with conversation, I paddled upstream along the tangled shoreline, hoping at least to spot a brookie darting to or from a lair where we might visit later, but no. Instead, we hauled the canoe over the first beaver dam, a short but sturdy wall of dirt and timbers that held

A VIEW INTO THE UPPER PONDS

back the water on two sides of a small island, then paddled toward the uppermost ponds to explore. There, a series of three more dams stair-step, each above each, shallower, more tangled and narrower as they go. About a half mile up, the ponds narrow to nothing more than a tangle of blown down trees and bramble bushes beside tall cedars that canopy a cool stream of water the width of an average boy's broad jump.

We hefted the canoe over the first dam and paddled around a short bend into a wide shallow, shaped like a large teardrop, too shallow to hold fish and barely deep enough for us to make way, its bottom lush with luminous, almost fluorescent waves of feathered algae, like angel hair, mermaid hair, growing only inches under the surface but spread across the entire pond, like nothing I'd seen before. We were luxuriant in our pace, abandoning the fly rod and sauntering so we might observe, barely making way in its slight current, and noting how distinct this pond was from the deeper, more silt-bottomed pools below. In time, we slid up the right side to the top of the pool along the only submerged log in the current, scattering about a half dozen fingerling trout, then nosed the canoe into the backside of the third dam, an ancient dam, so old the bottom four feet of timbers set there by beavers generations earlier had decayed into dirt, making a solid earth embankment four feet tall.

The deepest water is often on the upstream side of dams like this where often the largest fish will hold. It is sometimes possible to stand behind the dam, your profile below the trout's window of view, and cast stealthily up and over the dam. So before hauling the canoe up, we peeked over, only to find the surface covered with a musty green-brown algae floating on the surface, backed up for 15 feet or more, looking like a warm, week-old head on a heavy malt beer. So we pulled the canoe over and paddled up past the floaties, forgetting fishing altogether, finding instead a kind of freshwater kelp rising up from the bottom, a species I'd never seen. Dense stalks, about the diameter of a quarter and no more than a few inches apart, they clogged

A VIEW INTO THE UPPER PONDS

the entire right side of the pool and seemed to be the source of the musty algae we'd paddled through. On the left, and farther ahead, storm-tossed trees uprooted by an intense summer storm had all been slammed over, parallel, side by side, their entangled limbs forming a gauntlet for the canoe and rendering the pond nearly impossible to fish with dry flies. But I noticed deep holes where the roots had been torn up, and directed a few long rejected casts at the bases of these stumps as we crept forward. Then we both stopped, staring into the water.

Below us, at the bottom of the pond, an inexplicably beautiful and chilling life form — an algae — eye at the bottom of the pond — rusty orange and strangely gelatinous at the center, then fibrous and fluorescent around the edges, surrounded by and as if communicating with the same luminous, feathery green algae we'd seen in the lower dam. Our reflections and those of the terrestrial world wavered on the surface. We stayed a long time, almost afraid to poke it with a paddle, not wanting to break the spell of its presence there, grinning at each other and speechless — witnesses to the secret, silent life of this watery cosmos.

Afterward, we pulled ashore finding grey, green, bright red and amber lichens and mosses and fungi, all clinging to bare rock faces and to tree limbs and trunks, cushioning our footsteps over billion year old bedrock. The largest, clumped like cauliflower, I read later were over 50 years old, clinging tenaciously through the ravages of winter so it might emerge and thrive before our eyes.

Since boyhood I've canoed and waded and swum and submerged myself in lakes and ponds and rivers day and night, naked and clothed, open-eyed and masked with fins and snorkels; I've prodded and peered into currents, even crept up to undercut banks to try stroking long, secretive underbellies of trout, and caught fish with my bare hands. I've emerged leech-bitten and gasped once as a snapping turtle swam between my legs. My flies have accidentally caught bats and dragonflies, a two-foot water snake and a twenty-pound carp, its scales the size

A VIEW INTO THE UPPER PONDS

of quarters and a kind of ancient shelf-fungus on its sides; I've been tormented by every kind of biting bug and the sudden smack of beaver tails at night like anvils dropped from five-story buildings, and raccoons fighting in the black canopy above my head and wild turkey squawking into flight. I've dipped nets and cast lines and held voracious pike and helpless trout and seen the struggling eyes of animals whose lives remain as much a mystery to me as the deepest realms of space. So when I saw the delicate, luscious and mutable hues of the brook trout from Voelker's pond, and again, the inexplicable algae in the upper ponds, I could not help compare the billion-dollar images the Hubble telescope retrieved from the darkest points of deep space, a focal point "the size of a grain of salt at arm's length." There, scientists discovered a million or more galaxies — galaxies — each as large and larger than our own...

That evening, as the sun lit the mirrored pond ablaze, I gazed along the length of water, a stranger to the secret life beneath its surface. Then, like a

THE VOELKER'S POND ESSAYS

truce, I let the questions be, and simply, silently, worshiped.

A young John Voelker

A SEASON'S SENDOFF

THE VOELKER'S POND ESSAYS

A SEASON'S SEND OFF

A week before Indian summer kept temperatures in the 70's, and by afternoon enough grasshoppers, beetles, and other winged terrestrials hazarded into the water to stir up some good fishing. There had even been a sudden burst of feeding at dusk, tailing off at dark when we paddled in for the night.

But now the last day of the season had arrived and the night before the first serious forces of autumn swooped down from Canada in a single blow that meteorologists might call an "Alberta Clipper," but locals are more likely to call a "Canadian Crap Hammer." Gale force winds led a lightning-blazed, mop-bucket downpour, passing over the peninsula

A SEASON'S SEND OFF

like a cold angry hand, wiping away the warmth of Indian summer for good. Then overnight a hard, frosty stillness iced the windows of our cars and the clouds blew off, chilling the temperature down in the morning and killing off insect activity and trout feeding all day.

Perhaps it's because the pond's springs seep up from aquifers so cold and deep the weather we fishermen use to predict the fishing is virtually irrelevant to the creatures below. Or perhaps it's because the fish food in Voelker's pond takes mostly subsurface forms and follows cryptic codes of conduct we'll never fully decipher. No matter, it's clear the pond, like any fascinating, complicated personality, shows us only what it wants to, the face that meets the faces. After a lifetime on the pond Voelker himself could not explain its moods beyond the fact that the pond offered only a silent, blank stare with dark coming on fast.

But it is the pond's notorious moodiness that, ironically, can inspire hope, because it may decide at any time to break all rules of engagement, and offer up a lovely trout at the damnedest time, under the goofiest conditions. Or not.

Still, though a fisherman might not recognize (or even see) the insects the trout feed on, from May through August he can pretty much anticipate morning hatches to be followed by terrestrial activity in the afternoon, and occasional evening hatches, after which the pond shuts down for the night so fishermen can stare at the stars or sit around the campfire smoking cigars and reading selections from *Danny and the Boys* and *Trout Magic* out loud, laughing until they wet themselves.

But I'd never bothered fishing the pond at night — having never heard a rise after dark — and because it's common knowledge that brook trout hide out at night. At least this is true of most brook trout on most streams in the Lower Peninsula — where they have an understandable reason. First, Lower Peninsula brookies tend to be small — averaging six or seven inches. Others may claim more success than I, but I'm giddy when I release 10-inchers and overjoyed with 12- and 13-inchers (this summer I

A SEASON'S SEND OFF

about fell over in glory when I landed and released a 15-incher). The difference is, below the Mackinac bridge, most brook trout have to share the water with brown trout, a species that in deeper rivers can grow over 20 and up to 30 inches long. Once matured like this, browns tend to hide all day and then prowl the streams at night, especially muggy nights in July and August after the mayfly hatches die down, seeking out big meals like baitfish, crayfish, even wayfaring mice — and certainly wayfaring brook trout. An eight-inch brook trout would make a nutritious hors-d'oeuvre for a mature brown. Thus, all but perhaps the few largest brook trout hide out until dawn on rivers like these. And on Voelker's pond in my experience, nighttime meant bedtime for brookies too, even though the fish there are safe from marauding browns.

Under a moonless sky, the temperature dropping, mist came off the water now. Mist on the water and cold nights are never productive, but suddenly, a tremendous "glunk" echoed down the stream, a granddaddy rising, the largest I'd ever heard on this pond, the mythical fish Voelker claimed to have caught by accident once while competing with his friends, trying quickly to reel in a smaller trout when the big one hit.

At least he sounded upstream, perhaps in the hollow beyond the weed bed, and between the bramble-covered bank and sunken log. If only he would rise again I might locate him. So I waited. He must rise again, I thought. He will rise.

But nothing.

It was deep-hall dark, and the casting was dangerous — twigs and branches I could not see, but still I tried dragging flies, changing them three or four times and started casting blindly all over until finally hooking up on the weed bed, snagged solidly. Then, unbelievably, from far below, another "glunk" echoed over the pond, of equal magnitude.

"My Lord," I whimpered, scampering to release my hook and finally snapping off the fly, fumbling for my light and tying on a new one and casting blindly again for the longest time.

"It's over," I said, at last.

A SEASON'S SEND OFF

We lugged the canoe up and strapped it down on the car, cleaned up camp, put the paddles and rods away, made tea and walked down to the fire. And in the distance, echoing over the pond, "Glunk."

My jaw dropped.

"Look who gets the last word."

THE VOELKER'S POND ESSAYS

Voelker's sign on the way out

ACKNOWLEDGEMENTS

"Credentials of a Fishcar," "The Meanie Remains," "A Legacy of Setters," "Echoes," and "The Age We Season" all were initially published in *Traverse, The Magazine*. "Two-Hearted Hemingway" was originally published in the *Dunes Review*.

To my good friend, David Payne, for assisting me in the production of this book.

To Adam Tsaloff for use of his photos.

To Tim Schultz for the cover photo (check out his blog: UPTrout.com).

To my wife, Lisa, for her love and support; and to my lovely daughters, Meghan and Madison, my reasons for leaving a legacy behind.

Made in the USA
Lexington, KY
21 May 2018